# Andrew Brodie Basics

# LET'S DO SPELLING

### FOR AGES 6-7

- Over 400 words to practise and learn
- Regular progress tests
- Extra tips and brain booster questions

Published 2014 by Bloomsbury Publishing Plc
50 Bedford Square, London, WC1B 3DP

**www.bloomsbury.com**

ISBN 978-1-4729-0859-9

Copyright © 2014 Bloomsbury Publishing
Text copyright © 2014 Andrew Brodie
Cover and inside illustrations of Comma the Cat and Andrew Brodie © 2014 Nikalas Catlow
Other inside illustrations © 2014 Steve Evans

A CIP catalogue for this book is available from the British Library.

10 9 8 7 6 5 4 3 2 1

Printed in China by Leo Paper Products

This book is produced using paper that is made from wood grown in managed, sustainable forests. It is natural, renewable and recyclable. The logging and manufacturing process conform to the environmental regulations of the country of origin.

To see our full range of titles visit **www.bloomsbury.com**

B L O O M S B U R Y

# Notes for parents

## What's in this book

This is the second book in an exciting new series of *Andrew Brodie Basics: Let's Do Spelling*. Each book contains more than four hundred words especially chosen to boost children's confidence in spelling and to reflect the demands of the new National Curriculum.

During Key Stage 1, children are taught to read and write using a variety of approaches including phonics. They are encouraged to see the relationship between reading and spelling; 'blending' the sounds together to read them and 'segmenting' words by breaking them down into their sounds to spell them. You can help your child with this process when learning the spellings in this book. Of course, some words don't follow regular phonic patterns so your child will need to learn these 'tricky words' by looking at individual letters and the general shape of the word.

## How you can help

To get the most out of this book, take the time to discuss the activities with your child when there are no distractions around and they are in a responsive and enthusiastic mood. Talk through each of the practice words and what they mean by using them in spoken sentences, or by asking your child to make up sentences containing the words. Putting up posters of useful words around the house such as the days of the week and the months of the year, might also help with spelling generally.

To begin with, your child might find the spellings in this book quite tricky, but as they work their way through the activities and become familiar with the spelling patterns, their confidence should grow. The level of difficulty is increased gradually throughout the book but some spelling patterns are repeated to provide lots of opportunities for reinforcement and practice. Always be ready to provide plenty of encouragement and explain that they should learn from their mistakes rather than get disheartened.

## Look out for…

### Look, cover, write, check

Some pages feature 'Look, cover, write, check' exercises. Your child might have already come across this strategy in school. Ask your child to **look** carefully at each word, learning the shape of it and any letter patterns it contains. When they feel they know it, ask them to **cover** it with their hand or a piece of paper and to try writing it. They then look back at the original word and **write** it again to **check** that they really know it.

### Comma the Cat

Look out for Comma the Cat who tells your child which words to focus on for the progress test at the end of each section. You could help your child to learn these words by posting them around the house on sticky notes or writing them on flashcards for quick memory games.

### Brodie's Brain Boosters

*Brodie's Brain Boosters* feature quick extra activities designed to make your child think, using the skills and knowledge they already have. Some of these will ask your child to think of rhyming words. Don't worry if your child finds a rhyming word that doesn't match the spelling pattern of the given word. Use the opportunity to compare the spellings – looking carefully at words is, of course, the whole point of the activity!

### The answer section

The answer section at the end of this book can also be a useful learning tool. Ask your child to compare their spellings with the correct spellings provided on the answer pages. If they have spelt the words correctly, congratulate them, but if they haven't, don't let them worry about it! Instead, encourage them to learn the correct versions. Give lots of praise for any success.

# Jumbled Words

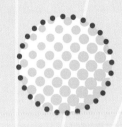

Put the letters in the right order to spell a word.
The first one has been done for you.

 chchru **church**

 chaco _____

 lcru _____

 soet _____

 senur _____

 kobo _____

 toba _____

 tofo _____

 dato _____

 doho _____

 nrub _____

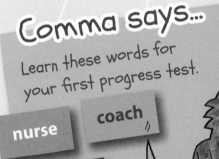

## Comma says...

Learn these words for your first progress test.

**nurse**  **coach**

**hood**

 toca _____

3

# Rhyming Words

Words that rhyme often have the same letter endings.

The word  rhymes with

Write the missing words and join them to the words that rhyme. The first one has been done for you.

___door___

bath

 **gold**

**floor**

colb

**last**

frnb

**honey**

Pust

**kind**

money

**path**

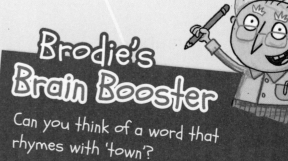
**Brodie's Brain Booster**
Can you think of a word that rhymes with 'town'?

4

# Sort the Words

**Read the words below.**

shower · plant · rain · stem · ice · flower

sunny · digging · thunder · snow · grow · soil

**Some of the words are about weather and some are about gardening.**
**Copy the words on to the correct list.**

## WEATHER WORDS

sunny

shower

rain

### Brodie's Brain Booster

One of our seasons is Autumn.
Can you name the other three seasons?

## GARDENING WORDS

Plant

digging

tuprebr

stem

### Comma says...

Learn these words for your first progress test.

digging · flower · shower

5

# Match the Words

Look at each picture and write the matching word next to it.
The first one has been done for you.

 ~~tray~~   ~~medal~~   plant   ~~sugar~~   ~~chimney~~   eye

 ~~bee~~   ~~sun~~   ~~glass~~   ~~two~~   water   ~~ball~~

 tray

 Plant

 two

 ball

 chimney

 eye

 methr

 wafr

 Supar

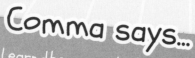 bee

 sun

medal

## Comma says...
Learn these words for your first progress test.

**chimney**   **water**   **sugar**

# Write the Words

Always use your best handwriting!

Read the words on the list.

Cover each word and see if you can write it without looking.
Then check and write it again.

| LOOK (THEN COVER) | WRITE | CHECK |
|---|---|---|
| annoy | | |
| royal | | |
| enjoy | | |
| enjoying | | |
| June | | |
| tune | | |
| start | | |
| smart | | |
| park | | |
| spark | | |
| dream | | |
| reach | | |

Comma says...

Learn these words for your first progress test.

annoying    tune

dream

Brodie's Brain Booster

Can you think of a word that rhymes with 'spark' ?

**Write the words in the gaps.**

**1** The _____ was a rose .

**2** Smoke was rising from the _____ .

**3** The teacher was very _____ when she gave the children some apples.

**4** There was a short _____ of rain.

**5** The woman was _____ her garden.

**The letters in these words are mixed up.**
**Can you put them in the righ   t order?**

> Use the words you have practised.

**6** terwa _____

**7** eymon _____

**8** hodo _____

**9** chcoa _____

**10** garsu _____

**Write the words in the gaps.**

**11** The cup fell on to the _____ .

**12** The doctor and the _____ looked after me.

**13** Sometimes my sister is very _____ .

**14** The song has a lovely _____ .

**15** Last night I had a bad _____ .

Score ___ / 15

# Jumbled Words

Put the letters in the right order to spell a word.
The first one has been done for you.

 low    *owl*

 30 tythir _____

 woc _____

 cleric _____

 thomu _____

 13 teenriht _____

 owncr _____

 loga _____

 epi _____

 ceaf _____

 eti _____

 ohues _____

# Rhyming Words

Words that rhyme often have the same letter endings.

The word **blue** rhymes with **glue**.

Write the missing words and join them to the words that rhyme.

| blue | cried | charge | bridge | mice | race |

large

tried

lace

fridge

glue

nice

## Comma says...
Learn these words for your second progress test.

charge    bridge

tried

## Brodie's Brain Booster
Can you think of a word that rhymes with 'hedge'?

# Sort the Words

**Read the words below.**

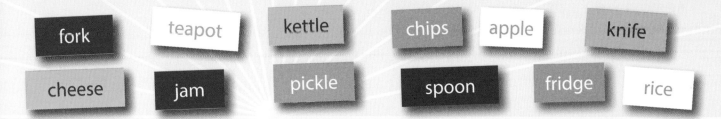

| fork | teapot | kettle | chips | apple | knife |
|------|--------|--------|-------|-------|-------|

| cheese | jam | pickle | spoon | fridge | rice |
|--------|-----|--------|-------|--------|------|

**Some of the words are types of food and some are kitchen things.**
**Copy the words on to the correct list.**

## FOOD WORDS

_____

_____

_____

_____

_____

_____

**Brodie's**
**Brain Booster**
Can you spell out loud the name of another item that is used for cooking?

## KITCHEN THINGS

_____

_____

_____

_____

_____

_____

_____

**Comma says...**
Learn these words for your second progress test.

| apple | knife |
|-------|-------|

kettle

11

# Match the Words

Look at each picture and write the matching word next to it.
The first one has been done for you.

badge    candle    ~~winter~~    wood    table    circle

giraffe    jar    camper    jaw    badger    ice

winter

**Comma says...**
Learn these words for your second progress test.

winter    badger    table

# Write the Words

Read the words on the list.

Cover each word and see if you can write it without looking. Then check and write it again.

| LOOK (THEN COVER) | WRITE | CHECK |
|---|---|---|
| true | | |
| clue | | |
| rescue | | |
| drew | | |
| threw | | |
| fried | | |
| crowd | | |
| brown | | |
| dodge | | |
| fudge | | |
| budge | | |
| fancy | | |

## Comma says...

Learn these words for your second progress test.

**true**  **crowd**

**dodge**

## Brodie's Brain Booster

Can you think of a word that rhymes with 'knock'?

13

**Write the words in the gaps.**

**1** The _____ flew silently.

**2** The dentist asked me to open my _____ very wide.

**3** There is a _____ over the river.

**4** The teacher told us a _____ story.

**5** A stone was heading straight for me so I had to _____ it.

**The letters in these words are mixed up.
Can you put them in the right order?**

Use the words you have practised.

**6** gerbad _____

**7** kleett _____

**8** pplea _____

**9** balet _____

**10** finke _____

**Write the words in the gaps.**

**11** A huge _____ watched the football match.

**12** Sometimes it snows in the _____ .

**13** The lady didn't _____ me to have a ride on the horse because it was free.

**14** I _____ to catch the ball but I dropped it.

**15** A _____ is round.

Score _____ /15

# Jumbled Words

Put the letters in the right order to spell a word.
The first one has been done for you.

touba **about**

 lebott _____

 lemac _____

 lesadd _____

 lowet _____

 wap _____

 leadm _____

 wany _____

 delap _____

 lacw _____

 lepadd _____

 lepudd _____

## Comma says...

Learn these words for your third progress test.

about    paddle

yawn

# Rhyming Words

Words that rhyme often have the same letter endings.

The word care rhymes with dare .

Write the missing words and join them to the words that rhyme.

| there | care | full | ear | push | school |

cool

pull

where

bush

dare

near

**Comma says...**
Learn these words for your third progress test.

school   where

care

**Brodie's Brain Booster**
Can you think of a word that rhymes with 'written'?

16

# Sort the Words

**Read the words below.**

hiking  changed  crying  hiked  changing  cried

liked  knitted  copying  liking  knitting  copied

**Some of the words end with 'ing' and some end with 'ed'.**
**Copy the words on to the correct list.**

## WORDS ENDING WITH 'ing'

_____

_____

_____

_____

_____

_____

**Brodie's Brain Booster**

Can you spell the ing word and the ed word that go with the word 'peep'?

## WORDS ENDING WITH 'ed'

_____

_____

_____

_____

_____

_____

**Comma says...**

Learn these words for your third progress test.

copying  copied  copy

# Match the Words

Look at each picture and write the matching word next to it.
The first one has been done for you.

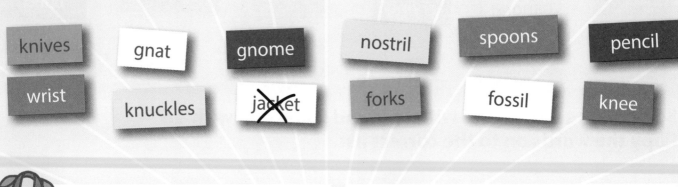

knives    gnat    gnome    nostril    spoons    pencil

wrist    knuckles    ~~jacket~~    forks    fossil    knee

jacket

Comma says...

Learn these words for your third progress test.

knives    pencil

jacket

# Write the Words

Read the words on the list.

Cover each word and see if you can write it without looking.
Then check and write it again. All of them start with silent letters.

| LOOK (THEN COVER) | WRITE | CHECK |
| --- | --- | --- |
| write | | |
| writing | | |
| written | | |
| wrote | | |
| wrap | | |
| wrapping | | |
| wrapped | | |
| knock | | |
| knocked | | |
| knocking | | |
| know | | |
| kneel | | |

## Comma says...

Learn these words for your third progress test.

writing    wrapped    knocking

## Brodie's Brain Booster

Can you think of a word that rhymes with 'cable'?

**Write the words in the gaps.**

**1** I was cross because the boy next to me _____ all my work.

**2** "You should not _____ my work," I said to him.

**3** "I am not _____ your work," he replied.

**4** I was busy _____ my story.

**5** Then the boy snatched my _____ so I couldn't write any more!

**The letters in these words are mixed up.
Can you put them in the right order?**

> Use the words you have practised.

**6** nwya _____

**7** jeckat _____

**8** knevis _____

**9** knongick _____

**10** loosch _____

**Write the words in the gaps.**

**11** The teacher told us _____ her holiday.

**12** She said that she loves to _____ in the sea.

**13** She likes to go to places _____ the sun shines every day.

**14** This year the sun did not shine very much and our teacher had to stay _____ up in warm clothes.

**15** She says that next year she is going to take more _____ when she plans her holiday.

**Score** _____ / 15

20

# Jumbled Words

Put the letters in the right order to spell a word.
The first one has been done for you.

 hendal **handle**

 trissa _____

 eeeldn _____

 riha _____

 jengul _____

 nepho _____

 lyf _____

 phonlid _____

 yabb _____

 leweh _____

 ekib _____

 richa _____

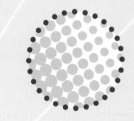

# Rhyming Words

Words that rhyme often have the same letter endings.

The word `funny` rhymes with `sunny`.

Write the missing words and join them to the words that rhyme.

happy   shove   mask   some   lorry   sunny

funny

snappy

sorry

love

come

ask

**Comma says...**

Learn these words for your fourth progress test.

sorry   shove

funny

**Brodie's Brain Booster**

Can you think of a word that rhymes with 'when'?

22

# Sort the Words

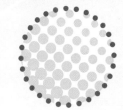

Read the words below. Some of the words end with 'ing' and some end with 'ed'. Copy the words on to the correct list.

potted    slipping    shopping    potting    patted    shopped

dripping    spotted    patting    dripped    slipped    spotting

**Copy the words on to the correct list:**

**WORDS WITH 'ing'**

_____

_____

_____

_____

_____

_____

### Brodie's Brain Booster

Can you spell the 'ing' word and the 'ed' word that go with the word 'drop'?

**WORDS WITH 'ed'**

_____

_____

_____

_____

_____

### Comma says...

Learn these words for your fourth progress test.

**shopping**    **spotted**

**dripping**

# Match the Words

Look at each picture and write the matching word next to it.
The first one has been done for you.

road (crossed out)    tunnel    orange    hospital    vegetables    squirrel

juice    animals    food    tinsel    cattle    babies

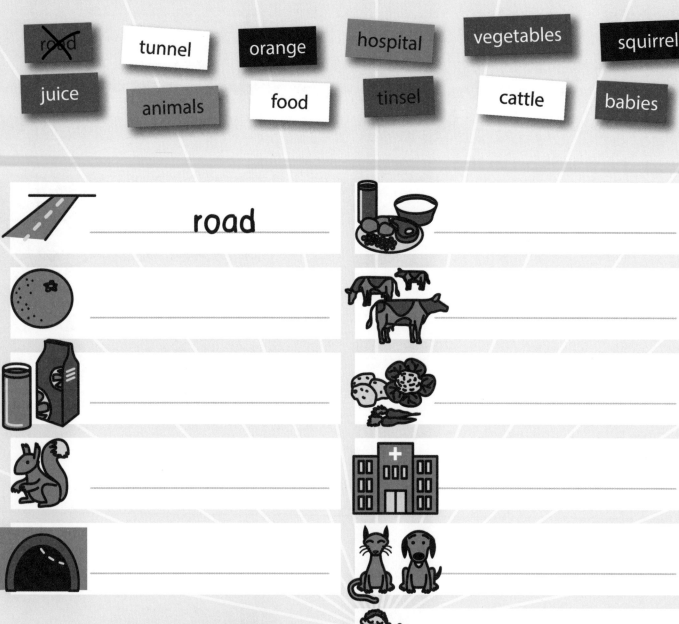

road

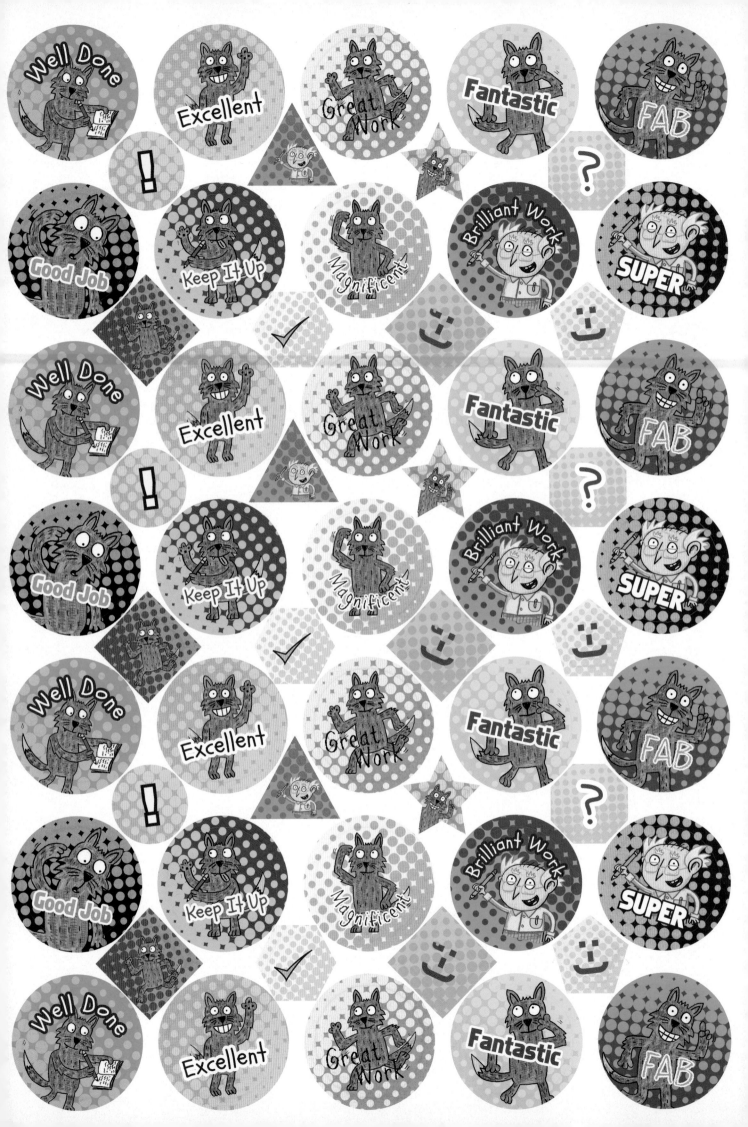

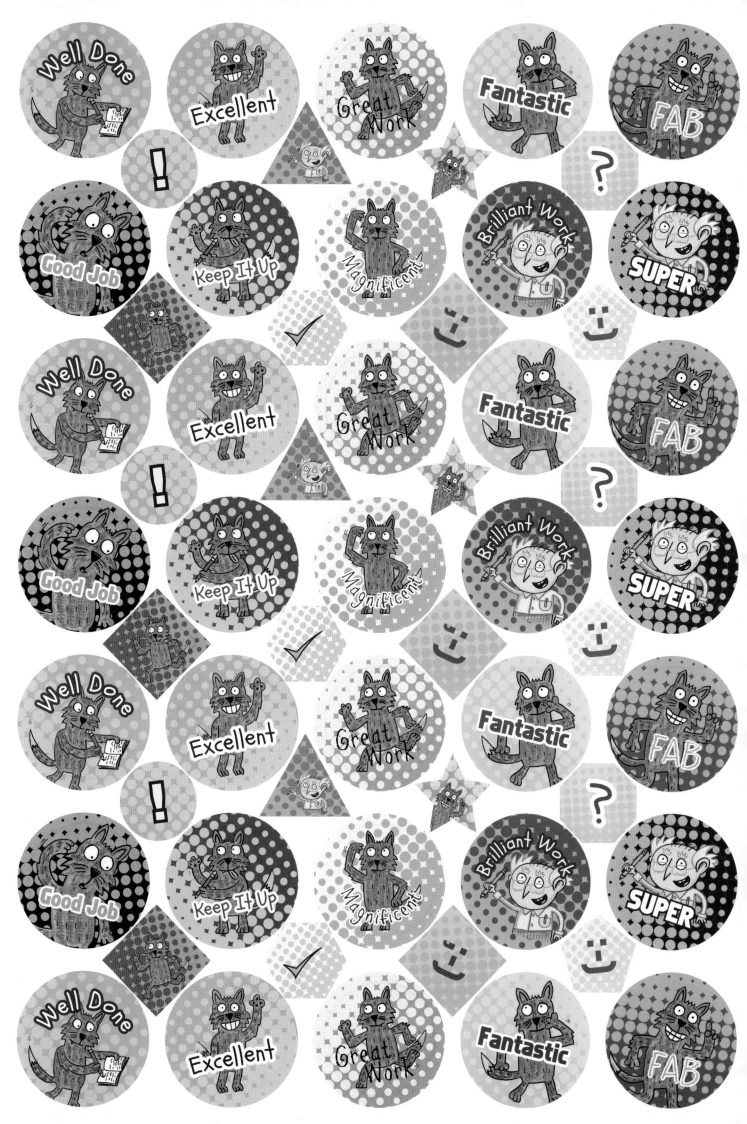

# Write the Words

Read the words on the list.

Cover each word and see if you can write it without looking. Then check and write it again.

| LOOK (THEN COVER) | WRITE | CHECK |
| --- | --- | --- |
| took | | |
| look | | |
| looking | | |
| looked | | |
| cook | | |
| cooking | | |
| cooked | | |
| good | | |
| better | | |
| best | | |
| count | | |
| loud | | |

## Comma says...

Learn these words for your fourth progress test.

looked    better    count

## Brodie's Brain Booster

Can you think of a word that rhymes with 'loud'?

**Write the words in the gaps.**

1. The train went into a dark _____ .

2. I _____ everywhere for my favourite teddy.

3. It is not nice to _____ people over.

4. "You should say _____ ," said the boy.

5. I go _____ with my mum to buy our food.

**The letters in these words are mixed up.**
**Can you put them in the right order?**

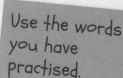

Use the words you have practised.

6. leweh _____

7. ybab _____

8. sibabe _____

9. hirca _____

10. ceiju _____

**Write the words in the gaps.**

11. The joke was very _____ .

12. I _____ an ice-cream van in the distance.

13. The tap is annoying because it keeps _____ .

14. I like milk but I think orange juice is _____ .

15. I can _____ to over a hundred.

**Score** ___ / 15

# Jumbled Words

Put the letters in the right order to spell a word.

The first one has been done for you.

 seorh **horse**

 mrud _____

 deri _____

 blmic _____

 gjo _____

 lawk _____

 ktal _____

Write an 'ing' word for each of the pictures below.

 _____

 _____

 _____

 _____

 _____

## Comma says...

Learn these words for your fifth progress test.

horse    climbing

talking

# Rhyming Words

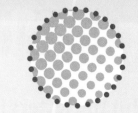

Words that rhyme often have the same letter endings.

The word `walking` rhymes with `talking`.

Write the missing words and join them to the words that rhyme.

mopping     hopped     talked     hummed     talking     station

walking

walked

shopping

stopped

nation

drummed

## Comma says...

Learn these words for your fifth progress test.

shopping     station     walking

## Brodie's Brain Booster

Can you think of a word that rhymes with 'stopping'?

# Sort the Words

**Read the words below.**

televisions    classes    hours    fly    television    worm

hour    class    worms    glasses    flies    glass

**Some of the words are singular and some are plural.**
**Copy the words on to the correct list.**

## SINGULAR WORDS

_____

_____

_____

_____

_____

_____

_____

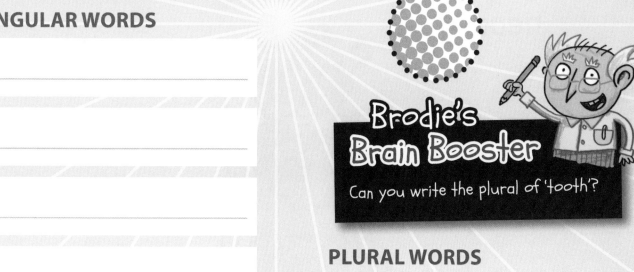

## Brodie's Brain Booster

Can you write the plural of 'tooth'?

## PLURAL WORDS

_____

_____

_____

_____

_____

_____

_____

## Comma says...

Learn these words for your fifth progress test.

television    glasses    hour

# Match the Words

Look at the picture and write the matching words.

The first one has been done for you.

elbow  he~~ad~~  shoulder  knee  foot  neck

eye  ear  mouth  nose  eyebrow  fingers

1
head

2

3

4

5

6

7

8

9

10

11

12

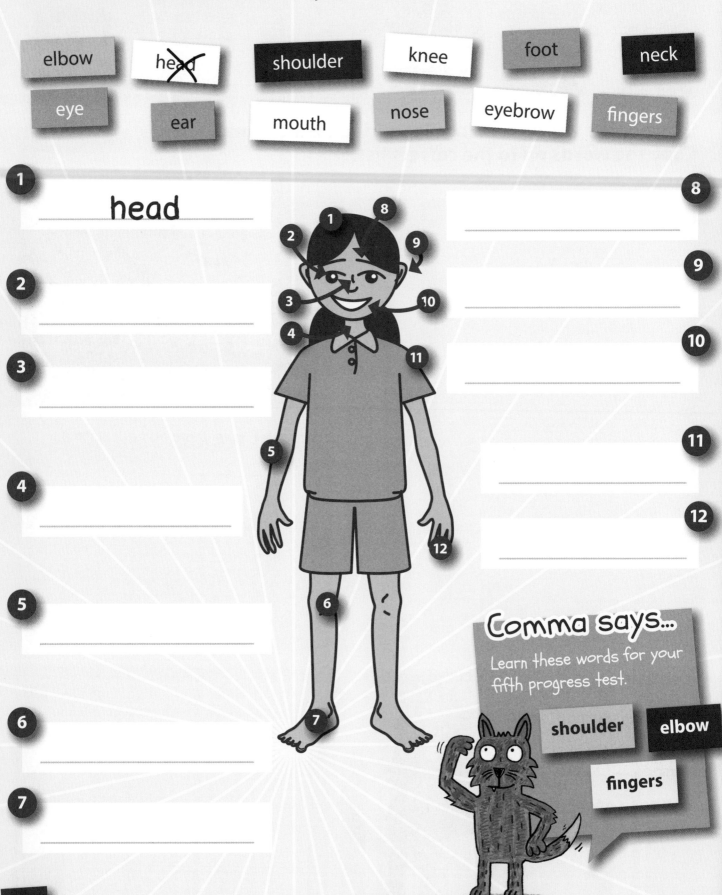

# Write the Words

Always use your best handwriting!

Read the words on the list.

Cover each word and see if you can write it without looking.
Then check and write it again.

| LOOK (THEN COVER) | WRITE | CHECK |
|---|---|---|
| call | | |
| hall | | |
| wall | | |
| tall | | |
| calling | | |
| called | | |
| always | | |
| sometimes | | |
| never | | |
| nice | | |
| nicer | | |
| nicest | | |

## Comma says...

Learn these words for your fifth progress test.

**calling**   **always**

**sometimes**

## Brodie's Brain Booster

Can you think of a word that rhymes with 'hiker'?

**Write the words in the gaps.**

1  The girl is _____ a tree.

2  The children are _____ .

3  The girl is _____ , not running.

4  We put the food in the _____ trolley.

5  I like watching _____ .

**The letters in these words are mixed up.
Can you put them in the right order?**

Use the words you have practised.

6  seroh _____

7  sseglas _____

8  resgfin _____

9  lobew _____

10  tionsta _____

**Write the words in the gaps.**

11  There are sixty minutes in an _____ .

12  There is a parrot on the pirate's _____ .

13  My mum was _____ my name.

14  I _____ go to school on Mondays, except in the holidays.

15  I _____ have jam on my toast.

**Score** _____ /15

# Jumbled Words

Put the letters in the right order to spell a word.
One has been done for you.

**5** thfif ................................

**1** rtsif ...... first ......

**6** thixs ................................

**3** dirth ................................

**7** venseth ................................

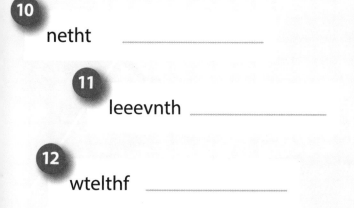

**2** sconed ................................

**4** frouth ................................

**9** thnin ................................

**8** igehth ................................

**10** netht ................................

**11** leeevnth ................................

**12** wtelthf ................................

# Rhyming Words

Words that rhyme often have the same letter endings.

The word `hold` rhymes with `told`.

Write the missing words and join them to the words that rhyme.

`told`   `any`   `prove`   `calf`   `could`   `badly`

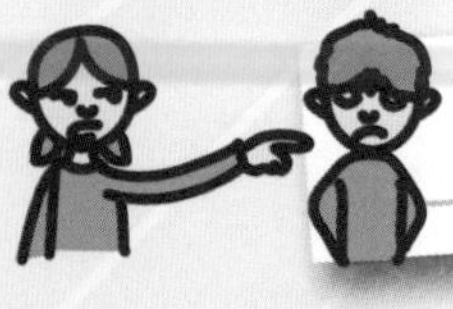

**sadly**

**half**

**many**

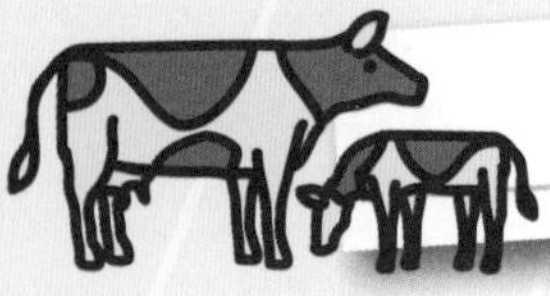

**should**

**hold**

**move**

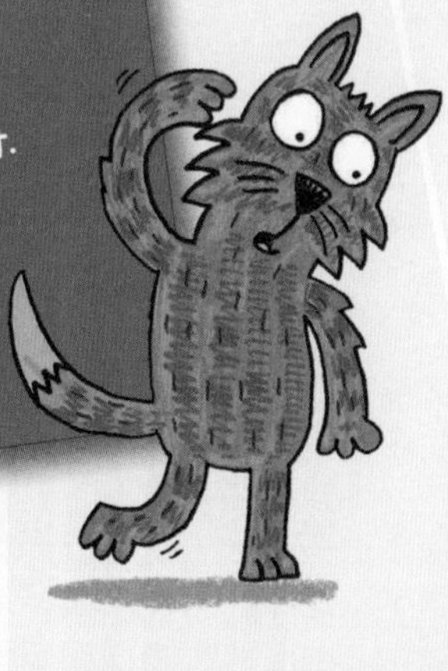

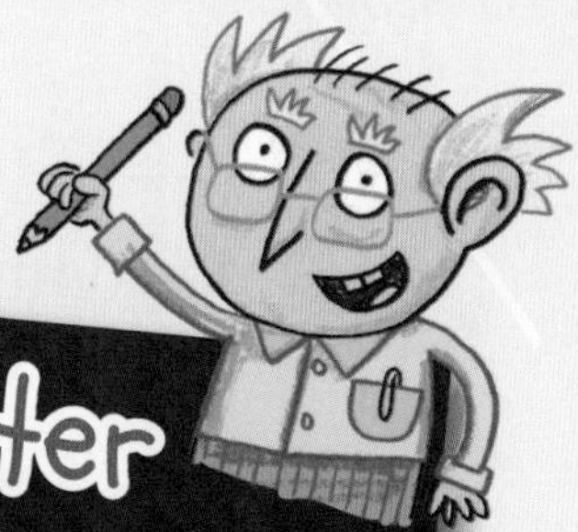

## Brodie's Brain Booster

Can you think of another word that rhymes with 'could' and 'should'?

# Sort the Words

**Read the words below.**

pound   world   town   spend   fort   coins

port   notes   village   purse   penny   city

**Some of the words are about money and some
are about places. Copy the words on to the correct list.**

## WORDS ABOUT MONEY

_____

_____

_____

_____

_____

_____

## WORDS ABOUT PLACES

_____

_____

_____

_____

_____

Comma says...
Learn these words for
your sixth progress test.

pound   village   world

# Match the Words

Look at each picture and write the matching word next to it.
The first one has been done for you.

clothes   coat   trousers   ~~vest~~   shirt   dress

socks   tie   skirt   belt   shorts   scarf

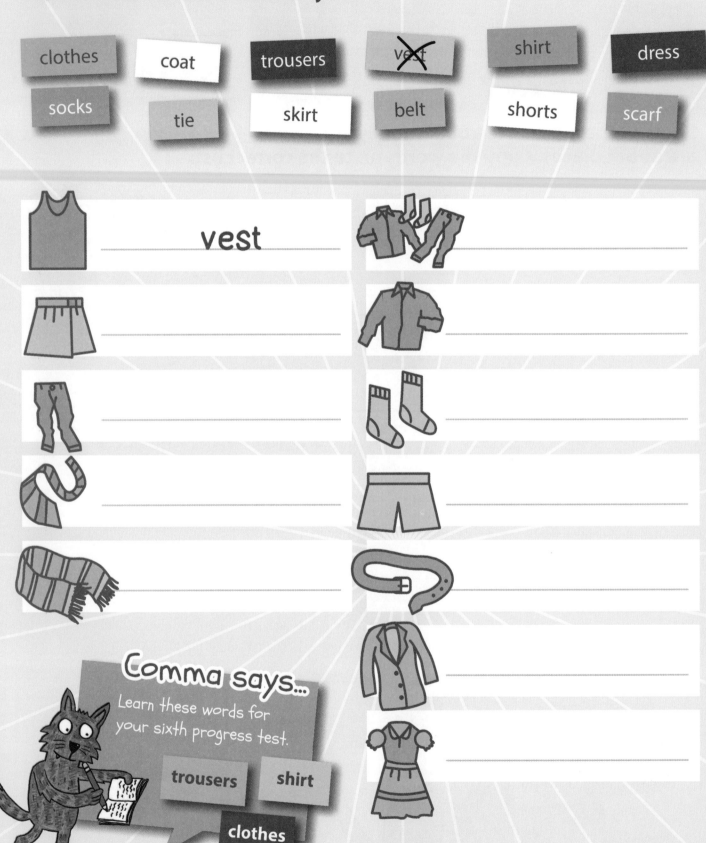

vest

**Comma says...**
Learn these words for your sixth progress test.

trousers   shirt

clothes

36

# Write the Words

Always use your best handwriting!

Read the words on the list.

Cover each word and see if you can write it without looking. Then check and write it again.

| LOOK (THEN COVER) | WRITE | CHECK |
|---|---|---|
| every | | |
| everybody | | |
| even | | |
| great | | |
| most | | |
| only | | |
| mind | | |
| behind | | |
| can't | | |
| didn't | | |
| want | | |
| watch | | |

**Comma says...**
Learn these words for your sixth progress test.

every    behind

didn't

**Brodie's Brain Booster**
Can you think of a word that rhymes with 'couldn't'?

**Write the words in the gaps.**

**1** August is the _____ month of the year.

**2** February is the _____ month of the year.

**3** December is the _____ month of the year.

**4** I go to school in _____ month except August.

**5** There are twelve months in a whole year. There are six months in

_____ a year.

**The letters in these words are mixed up.**
**Can you put them in the right order?**

Use the words you have practised.

**6** dopun _____

**7** rhist _____

**8** serstrou _____

**9** dorwl _____

**10** locesth _____

**Write the words in the gaps.**

**11** Some people live in a town and some people live in a small _____ .

**12** My mum said I _____ go and play with my friend.

**13** She said I _____ take some chocolate for both of us.

**14** I found my toy _____ the sofa.

**15** I _____ have any pudding because I was too full.

**Score** ____ /15

# Jumbled Words

I have mixed up some letters. Can you write the words for me?

Put the letters in the right order to spell a word.

The first one has been done for you.

| | |
|---|---|
| unaaJyr | January |
| yreFruba | |
| cahrM | |
| lirpA | |
| aMy | |
| uJen | |
| lyuJ | |

| | |
|---|---|
| stugAu | |
| tebSepemr | |
| berOcot | |
| vemNoreb | |
| bercemDe | |

## Comma says...

Learn these words for your seventh progress test.

**January** **February** **September**

39

# Rhyming Words

Words that rhyme often have the same letter endings.

The word muddle rhymes with puddle.

Write the missing words and join them to the words that rhyme.

puddle    fiddle    giggle    little    tickle    puzzle

muzzle

brittle

muddle

middle

wiggle

trickle

## Comma says...

Learn these words for your seventh progress test.

muddle    puzzles

tickle

## Brodie's Brain Booster

Can you think of a word that rhymes with 'snappier'?

# Sort the Words

**Read the words below.**

kitten    mouse    father    goat    donkey    mother

elephant    brother    children    monkey    sister    child

**Some of the words are people and some are animals.
Copy the words on to the correct list.**

## PEOPLE

_____

_____

_____

_____

_____

_____

### Brodie's Brain Booster

Can you think of an animal that is not in the list?

## ANIMALS

_____

_____

_____

_____

_____

_____

_____

### Comma says...

Learn these words for your seventh progress test.

**brother**    **sister**

**monkey**

41

# Match the Words

Look at each picture and write the matching word next to it.
The first one has been done for you.

shield ~~shield~~     runner     football     light     playground     motorway

pavement     night     grass     field     treasure     giant

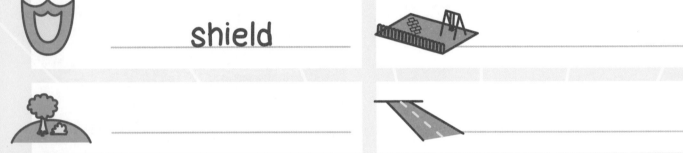

shield

_____

_____

_____

_____

_____

_____

_____

_____

_____

## Comma says...

Learn these words for your seventh progress test.

**field**    **playground**

**motorway**

# Write the Words

Always use your best handwriting!

Read the words on the list.

Cover each word and see if you can write it without looking. Then check and write it again.

| LOOK (THEN COVER) | WRITE | CHECK |
|---|---|---|
| bundle | | |
| tingle | | |
| single | | |
| cycle | | |
| travel | | |
| magic | | |
| gentle | | |
| energy | | |
| twice | | |
| terrible | | |
| horrible | | |
| carries | | |

## Comma says...

Learn these words for your seventh progress test.

energy  horrible

carries

## Brodie's Brain Booster

Can you think of a word that rhymes with 'twice'?

**Write the words in the gaps.**

1  The first month of the year is _____ .

2  The second month of the year is _____ .

3  Write the month that comes after August. _____

4  My sister likes to do jigsaw _____ .

5  Sometimes she gets all the pieces in a _____ .

**The letters in these words are mixed up. Can you put them in the right order?**

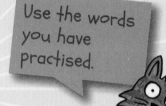

Use the words you have practised.

6  lifed      _____

7  keynom     _____

8  waymorot   _____

9  groundlayp _____

10 leckit     _____

**Write the words in the gaps.**

11 I have a little _____ .

12 I have a big _____ .

13 My brother runs around all day.  He has lots of _____ .

14 Sometimes my sister is _____ to me.

15 Sometimes she is kind and she _____ my bag for me.

**Score** ____ / 15

# ANSWERS

## Page 3 • Jumbled Words

| | |
|---|---|
| curl | coach |
| nurse | toes |
| boat | book |
| toad | foot |
| burn | hood |
| coat | |

## Page 4 • Rhyming Words

door rhymes with floor
bath rhymes with path
cold rhymes with gold
find rhymes with kind
fast rhymes with last
money rhymes with honey

Brain Booster:
brown, clown, frown, or any other rhyming word

## Page 5 • Sort the Words

| Weather words: | Words about gardening: |
|---|---|
| shower | plant |
| rain | stem |
| ice | flower |
| sunny | digging |
| thunder | grow |
| snow | soil |

Brain Booster:
Spring, Summer, Winter

## Page 6 • Match the Words

| | |
|---|---|
| plant | chimney |
| two | eye |
| ball | sugar |
| | glass |
| | water |
| | bee |
| | sun |
| | medal |

## Page 7 • Write the Words

words written as neatly as possible

Brain Booster:
mark, shark, dark, or any other rhyming word

## Page 8 • Progress Test 1

1. flower
2. chimney
3. kind
4. shower
5. digging

6. water
7. money
8. hood
9. coach
10. sugar

11. floor
12. nurse
13. annoying
14. tune
15. dream

## Page 9

| | |
|---|---|
| cow | thirty |
| mouth | circle |
| crown | thirteen |
| pie | goal |
| tie | face |
| house | |

## Page 10 • Rhyming Words

mice rhymes with nice
charge rhymes with large
race rhymes with lace
cried rhymes with tried
blue rhymes with glue
bridge rhymes with fridge

Brain Booster:
edge, ledge, or any other rhyming word

## Page 11 • Sort the Words

| Food words: | Kitchen things: |
|---|---|
| chips | fork |
| apple | teapot |
| cheese | kettle |
| jam | knife |
| pickle | spoon |
| rice | fridge |

Brain Booster:
saucepan, frying pan, oven, toaster, microwave, or any other appropriate word associated with cooking

## Page 12 • Match the Words

| | |
|---|---|
| camper | giraffe |
| wood | jar |
| badger | jaw |
| badge | ice |
| | table |
| | candle |
| | circle |

## Page 13 • Write the Words

words written as neatly as possible

Brain Booster:
lock, dock, clock, or any other rhyming word

## Page 14 • Progress Test 2

1. owl
2. mouth
3. bridge
4. true
5. dodge

6. badger
7. kettle
8. apple
9. table

10. knife
11. crowd
12. winter
13. charge
14. tried
15. circle

## Page 15 • Jumbled Words

camel
towel
medal
pedal
paddle
puddle

bottle
saddle
paw
yawn
claw

## Page 16 • Rhyming Words

ear rhymes with near
care rhymes with dare
there rhymes with where
full rhymes with pull
push rhymes with bush
school rhymes with cool

Brain Booster:

bitten, or any other rhyming word

## Page 17 • Sort the Words

| Words ending with 'ing': | Words ending with 'ed': |
|---|---|
| hiking | changed |
| crying | hiked |
| changing | cried |
| copying | liked |
| liking | knitted |
| knitting | copied |

Brain Booster:
peeping, peeped

## Page 18 • Match the Words

| forks | knives |
|---|---|
| wrist | spoons |
| knee | knuckles |
| fossil | pencil |
| | nostril |
| | gnat |
| | gnome |

## Page 19 • Write the Words

words written as neatly as possible

Brain Booster:
table, stable, able, or any other rhyming word

## Page 20 • Progress Test 3

1. copied
2. copy
3. copying
4. writing
5. pencil

6. yawn
7. jacket
8. knives
9. knocking
10. school

11. about
12. paddle
13. where
14. wrapped
15. care

## Page 21 • Jumbled Words

| needle | stairs |
|---|---|
| jungle | hair |
| fly | phone |
| baby | dolphin |
| bike | wheel |
| chair | |

## Page 22 • Rhyming Words

shove rhymes with love
happy rhymes with snappy
mask rhymes with ask
some rhymes with come
lorry rhymes with sorry
sunny rhymes with funny

Brain Booster:
then, hen, den, or any other rhyming word

## Page 23 • Sort the Words

| Words ending with 'ing': | Words ending with 'ed': |
|---|---|
| slipping | potted |
| shopping | patted |
| potting | shopped |
| dripping | spotted |
| patting | dripped |
| spotting | slipped |

Brain Booster:
dropping, dropped

## Page 24 • Match the Words

| orange | food |
|---|---|
| juice | cattle |
| squirrel | vegetables |
| | hospital |
| | animals |
| | babies |
| | tinsel |

## Page 25 • Write the Words

words written as neatly as possible

Brain Booster:
proud, cloud, or any other rhyming word (note that words such as 'crowd' are also acceptable)

## Page 26 • Progress Test 4

1. tunnel
2. looked
3. shove
4. sorry
5. shopping

6. wheel
7. baby
8. babies
9. chair
10. juice

11. funny
12. spotted
13. dripping
14. better
15. count

## Page 27 • Jumbled Words

| | |
|---|---|
| drum | drumming |
| ride | riding |
| climb | climbing |
| jog | walking |
| walk | talking |
| talk | |

## Page 28 • Rhyming Words

hopped rhymes with stopped
hummed rhymes with drummed
talking rhymes with walking
talked rhymes with walked
station rhymes with nation
mopping rhymes with shopping

Brain Booster:
hopping, shopping, or any other
rhyming word

## Page 29 • Sort the Words

| Singular words: | Plural words: |
|---|---|
| fly | televisions |
| television | classes |
| worm | hours |
| hour | worms |
| class | glasses |
| glass | flies |

Brain Booster:
teeth

## Page 30 • Match the Words

2. eye
3. nose
4. neck
5. elbow
6. knee
7. foot
8. eyebrow
9. ear
10. mouth
11. shoulder
12. fingers

## Page 31 • Write the Words

words written as neatly as
possible

Brain Booster:
biker

## Page 32 • Progress Test 5

1. climbing
2. talking
3. walking
4. shopping
5. television

6. horse
7. glasses
8. fingers
9. elbow
10. station

11. hour
12. shoulder
13. calling
14. always
15. sometimes

## Page 33 • Jumbled Words

1. second
2. third
3. fourth
4. fifth
5. sixth
6. seventh
7. eighth
8. ninth
9. tenth
10. eleventh
11. twelfth

## Page 34 • Rhyming Words

told rhymes with hold
any rhymes with many
prove rhymes with move
calf rhymes with half
could rhymes with should
badly rhymes with sadly

Brain Booster:
would
(note that words such as 'good'
and 'wood' are also acceptable)

## Page 35 • Sort the Words

| Words about money: | Words about places: |
|---|---|
| pound | world |
| spend | town |
| coins | fort |
| notes | port |
| purse | village |
| penny | city |

Brain Booster:
planets

## Page 36 • Match the Words

| | |
|---|---|
| skirt | clothes |
| trousers | shirt |
| tie | socks |
| scarf | shorts |
| | belt |
| | coat |
| | dress |

## Page 37 • Write the Words

words written as neatly as
possible

Brain Booster:
shouldn't, wouldn't

## Page 38 • Progress Test 6

1. eighth
2. second
3. twelfth
4. every
5. half

6. pound
7. shirt
8. trousers
9. world
10. clothes

11. village
12. could
13. should
14. behind
15. didn't

## Page 39 • Jumbled Words

| | |
|---|---|
| February | August |
| March | September |
| April | October |
| May | November |
| June | December |
| July | |

## Page 40 • Rhyming Words

puddle rhymes with muddle
giggle rhymes with wiggle
little rhymes with brittle
puzzle rhymes with muzzle
tickle rhymes with trickle
fiddle rhymes with middle

Brain Booster:
happier

## Page 41 • Sort the Words

| **People:** | **Animals:** |
|---|---|
| father | kitten |
| mother | mouse |
| brother | goat |
| children | donkey |
| sister | elephant |
| child | monkey |

Brain Booster:
any animal that is not on the list

## Page 42 • Match the Words

| | |
|---|---|
| field | playground |
| night | motorway |
| light | runner |
| football | treasure |
| | pavement |
| | grass |
| | giant |

## Page 43 • Write the Words

words written as neatly as
possible

Brain Booster:
mice, nice, advice, or any other
rhyming word

## Page 44 • Progress Test 7

1. January
2. February
3. September
4. puzzles
5. muddle

6. field
7. monkey
8. motorway
9. playground
10. tickle

11. brother
12. sister
13. energy
14. horrible
15. carries

Well done!
See you next time.

48